CW01372576

Hastings
in old picture postcards

by
Anne Scott

European Library – Zaltbommel/Netherlands

GB ISBN 90 288 5582 3 / CIP

© 1993 European Library – Zaltbommel/Netherlands

No part of this book may be reproduced in any form, by print, photoprint, microfilm or any other means, without written permission from the publisher.

INTRODUCTION

Hastings is a seaside town in East Sussex, known throughout the world for the battle which took place nearby in 1066. The modern resort is set against the backdrop of the only range of high sandstone cliffs in south-east England. Here the wooded ridge of the Weald runs into the sea, with flat marshlands to east and west. Archaeologists have found flint tools up to 10,000 years old in the area, evidence of a substantial pre-historic population. The East and West Hills on either side of the Old Town were both fortified during the Iron Age, about 2,000-2,500 years ago. The Romans had important iron working sites in the countryside around Hastings in the 2nd-4th centuries AD, especially at Beauport.

The origins of the actual town of Hastings are obscure. It appears to have been named after Jutish invaders in the ninth century. It was a regionally important town in late Saxon times, with its own mint. But the site of the settlement then is unknown. The most likely location is somewhere to the south of today's Old Town or the Castle, with the evidence having been swept away by the sea. Burials from the tenth century have been found on the edge of the East Hill, near the cliff railway, but most of the site has been lost by erosion.

Much of the town was granted to the Norman Abbey of Fecamp by King Cnut before the Norman conquest in 1066. It therefore seems natural that Duke William should make for Hastings as a safe base to launch his claim to the English throne. He re-fortified the West Hill and until the 14th century his Castle was being strengthened and repaired. Natural erosion and the cutting away of the cliff in the 1820s to build Pelham Crescent has reduced the Castle remains considerably. The Priory Valley to the west of the Castle is named after the 12th century Augustinian Priory that stood where Cambridge Gardens is today. The monks moved to Warbleton near Heathfield, at the beginning of the 15th century, after the Priory was said to have been damaged by storm and flood. The buildings later became incorporated into the Priory Farm. The medieval town of Hastings was concentrated in the Bourne Valley, and this is known as the 'Old Town' today. The oldest surviving building seems to be St. Clements Church dating from about 1380. The town was probably established here soon after the Battle of Hastings, although possibly nearer the sea. Both All Saints and St. Clements Churches were originally nearer the sea. From late Saxon times Hastings was a leading member of the Cinque Ports whose duty was to provide ships for the King until the Royal Navy was created in the 16th century. This gave Hastings a special status and power in England, with the Crown granting its inhabitants valuable privileges in return for their military service.

Hastings declined from the 16th century because it had no sheltered harbour. Only ports with this facility could take part in the new age of overseas trade. Hastings became primarily a fishing port, albeit an important one at times. Roads across the Weald were notoriously bad. The sea remained a major transport route right up until the railways were first established in this area in the early 1850s. In 1839 the mail coach was still taking eight hours to reach London from Hastings.

Old Hastings was transformed in the early 19th century when it suddenly became a fashionable seaside resort. Demand for housing grew and house plots were at a premium in the confined space of the Bourne Valley. The town was therefore forced to grow westward under the Castle Cliff from about 1810. The population of Hastings was 3,175 in 1801, 6,300 in 1821 and by 1901 it had risen to 65,528. The first bank was opened in 1791 and the first guide book produced in 1794. Hastings had many famous visitors; some in the line of duty like the Duke of Wellington, some seeking inspiration and a healthy climate such as the painter Dante Gabriel Rossetti.

The town's 19th century expansion gave Hastings and St. Leonards some architectural gems. The beautiful Regency Pelham Crescent, designed by Joseph Kay, was begun in 1824, Wellington Square in 1815, and James Burton's St. Leonards from 1828. Throughout the 19th century development spread inland. Eventually the villages of Hollington and Ore became part of the Borough. The building of the tram system in 1905 opened up much of the rural hinterland to speculative house building.

The railway came to Bo-Peep, St. Leonards in 1846. In 1851 the town's main station was built in the Priory Valley confirming this area as the town's future centre instead of the Bourne Valley. The heyday of seaside Hastings came in the 1860s-1880s. In 1881 Hastings had the second largest population of any seaside resort in Britain. But the town gradually declined from the 1890s as new attractions were not provided. The photographs in this book show a popular seaside resort in slow decline during the early years of the 20th century. In 1926 Sidney Little was appointed Borough Engineer and this marked Hastings' last period of major tourism investment.

The demands of the visitors and those of the fishermen have caused conflict over the years. Changes in the coastline and opportunities taken for sea front development on reclaimed shingle can be clearly seen from looking at old postcards. The area of the fishermen's beach today is much reduced from even 100 years ago. It is now occupied largely by attractions aimed at tourists. Nevertheless the fishing industry survives, and Hastings still has the largest beach-launched fleet of fishing boats in Britain. A new fishmarket was recently built on the beach. It seems sad that visitors to Hastings cannot take to the water. The excitement of a trip on one of the huge pleasure yachts or a steamer to Brighton are things of the past.

A major change in the last fifty years is the disappearance of many small shops and trades. The demands of the motor car have destroyed the heart of the 'Old Town', now split by the Bourne road. The pictures give little idea of the crushing poverty which existed alongside the fashionable resort. The world of Robert Tressell who wrote 'The Ragged Trousered Philanthropists' in the light of his experiences as a house painter in Hastings, was not immortalised in any holiday postcard. However now, as then, Hastings depends on visitors for the greater part of its economy. Today the town's chief attractions are its beautiful natural setting, some fine period architecture and the 'Old Town' with its fishing fleet. I am grateful to the following people for their help in preparing this book: David Padgham, Steve Peak, Brion Purdey, Paul Reed and Brian Scott.

Anne Scott

1. c1904. This junction of High Street, Old London Road and Harold Road was known as the 'Top of the Town'. Trams came to Hastings in 1905 and this was the terminus for the eastern side of the town. The streets of the Old Town were too narrow for trams, so the motor bus seen waiting here would connect this end of the Old Town with the Memorial. 'Mastins', a local department store, gave customers tokens that could be used on the trams. When the 'trackless trolley' buses replaced the trams in 1929 they ran through the Old Town. The 'market cross' seen here commemorates the accession of Edward VII, but was not the site of a market.

HIGH WICKHAM HASTINGS 51.

2. Torfield in the foreground is now allotments and wild life habitat. It was owned by Major Carlisle Sayer until 1934 when he gave it to the town on condition it would remain permanent open space. The 'market cross' can just be seen in the bottom right-hand corner of the picture. The correspondent on this card in 1918 mentions the decrease in drives out from Hastings, presumably because of the First World War.

OLD TOWN FROM WEST HILL

3. When Hastings became fashionable with visitors, at the end of the 18th century, every available space was built on. This picture c1905, gives some idea of the density of housing in the Old Town prior to the clearances which took place between 1923-1960. At the top left fishing nets are drying on the hillside. This supports the theory that the land on the slopes of the East Hill called the 'Minnis', was common land. Nets were dried here because of lack of space on the beach.

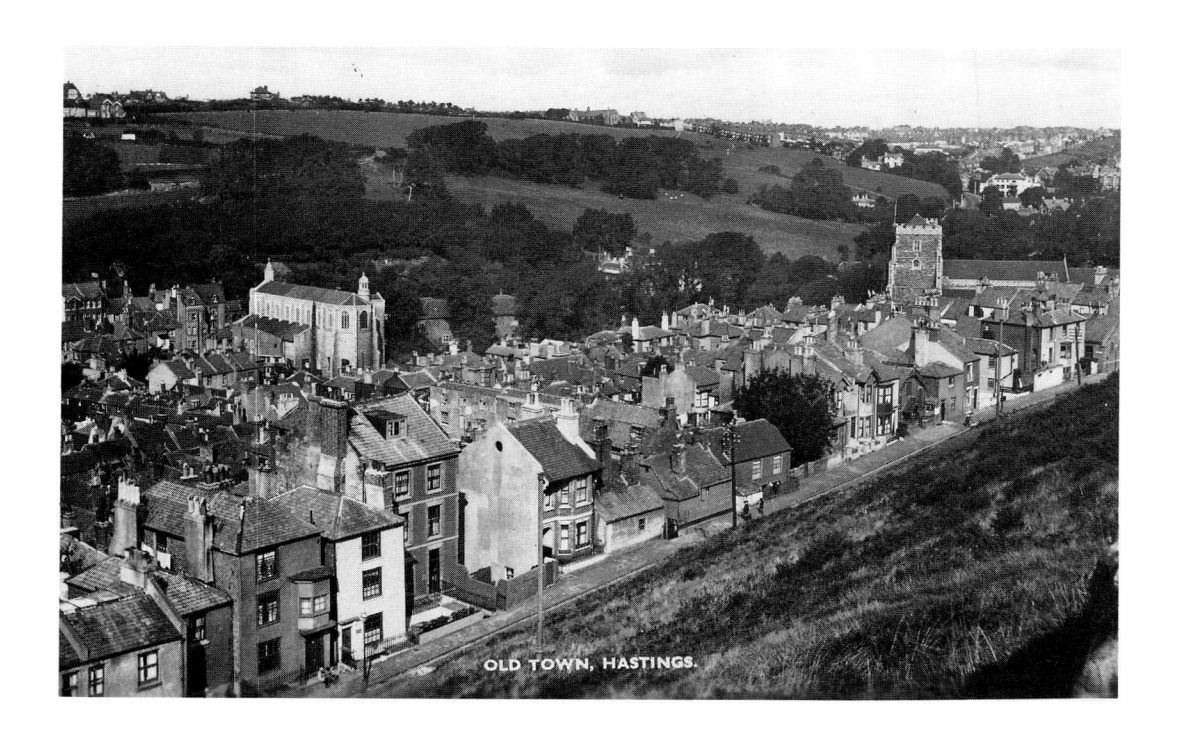

4. Taken about 1930, from the East Hill looking towards Priory Road. This picture shows the fields of Bembrook Farm before they were covered with houses to accommodate those displaced in the Old Town clearances. St. Clements Church Halton, demolished in 1970, can be seen in the centre on top of the hill. The church on the right of the picture is All Saints. The church just left of centre is St. Mary-Star-of-the-Sea, designed by Basil Champneys and built in 1882/83.

5. All Saints Street in about 1910. The high pavement was obviously not considered a danger then, as there are no railings. At this time there were twenty shops, three coal merchants and three schools in this street. This was the poor side of the Old Town, not the much sought after residential area it is today. In late August it was common to see carts being loaded up with household goods for the move out to the hop fields. Hop picking provided a much needed source of income and a welcome change of scene.

BOURNE WALK. HASTINGS. 720.

6. c1930. Bourne Walk was laid over the Bourne Stream after it was culverted in the 1830s. This area between High Street and All Saints Street was largely destroyed when the community was split by the clearances which began in the mid-1920s. These culminated in the construction of the Bourne Road in the early 1960s almost along the route of Bourne Walk. The town's prosperity had declined since the 19th century; the houses were small, old, crowded and in need of repair, but many fine vernacular buildings were lost in this great town planning blunder.

7. Bourne Street about 1890. The two houses outside which the pram is standing are said to be the oldest in Hastings. The building on the extreme left is the baths and wash house, opened in 1865.

681. HIGH STREET, OLD TOWN, HASTINGS. JUDGES'

8. High Street c1910. As in All Saints Street there were no railings on the high pavement before the Second World War. The sign on No. 93 'apartments', indicates a popular source of income. The building on the extreme right is the Roebuck Inn. The message on the back of the card reads: 'Great excitement here over the U-boat. The Town Crier says people may go aboard this afternoon.' Dated 16th April 1919.

9. This building is the 18th century Customs House in High Street, a relic of the days when Hastings was a port for customs purposes. The Customs Yard behind the gates on the left was used for storing seized smuggled goods and other items. It was demolished in 1962 despite attempts to preserve it, but the far end of the building with the long and short quoin stones, can still be seen attached to the Post Office on the right.

10. Hill Street looking towards St. Clements Church, where a curfew bell was rung during the winter at 8pm until the Second World War, a custom surviving from Norman times. This was the signal for the smaller boats to set off herring fishing. The Hole in the Wall pub is on the left of the picture. This was a greengrocers and off licence at this date c1905, but later became a pub which closed in 1971.

11. c1905. 'Stoakes and Carey' boot stores on the extreme right of the picture is now 'Ye Olde Pump House'. Next door was 'Henry Playfair and Co' another boot store. In 1910 George Street had six shoe shops and was a thriving commercial thoroughfare.

12. This picture c1930 shows Hastings and St. Leonards piers in the distance. The large corrugated iron coach station and the new boating lake can be seen top right. The build-up of shingle against the harbour since 1930 can be appreciated. The most dramatic elements of the picture are the horse capstans and the turning circles made by the horses, as the boats are hauled up the beach.

13. c1930. These two horses are working one of the capstans that hauled fishing boats out of the sea. The horses were hired from the Corporation stables at Rock-a-Nore by the fishermen. The Pierwarden collected the dues until this office disappeared in 1924. The Corporation replaced their horse-drawn dust carts with lorries in the mid-1930s, and motor winches then replaced the horse capstans. The net shops are unique to Hastings. They are mostly three-storied to accommodate three types of net, mackerel, herring and trawls. They were numbered in rows A-Z but now only L-W survive.

14. This fine photograph of the 1880s demonstrates how far west the fishing quarter then reached, and how many net shops have been lost. Hastings still has the largest beach-launched fleet in Britain. The East Hill lift has yet to be built.

15. c1905. A Hastings fishing boat drying its sails with a beam trawl over the side. Most of the boats on the water are Rye smacks. Hastings boats were too small to accommodate a steam engine. Motor engines were installed in boats here from 1914. In late Victorian times the fishing fleet totalled around 80 boats, today it is just over 40. Hastings boats are registered at Rye and the initials RX come from the first and last letters of 'Rye, Sussex'.

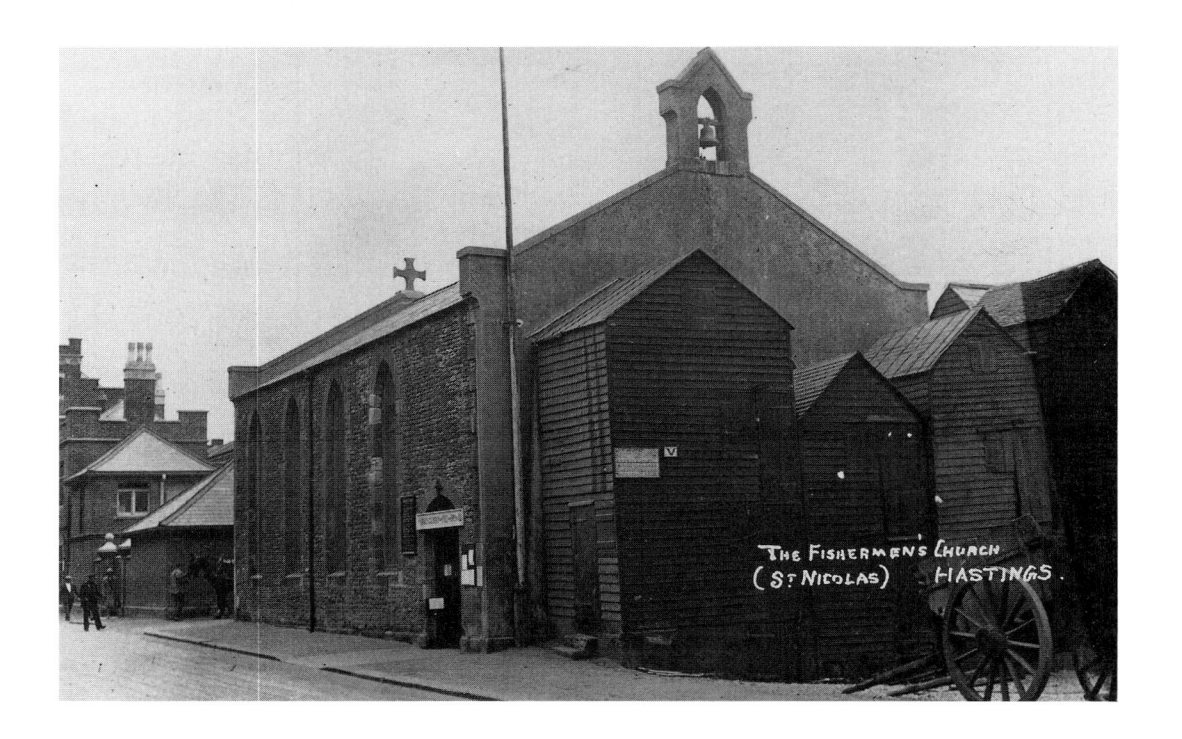

16. c1910. The Fishermen's Church, dedicated to the patron saint of fishermen St. Nicholas, was opened in 1854 as a Chapel of Ease for All Saints and St. Clements. It was used as a warehouse for a few years after 1945, before being opened as the Fishermen's Museum in 1956. The museum depicts the local fishing industry with a full-sized lugger on display. The church is still used for baptisms. A horse can be seen being led out of the Corporation stables to the left of the church, possibly to fix to the cart on the right or to work a capstan. The letter V can clearly be seen on the net shop indicating its row.

17. c1927. The buildings at Rock-a-Nore behind the boats have all been demolished, including the Cinque Port Artillery Volunteers Drill Hall with the square tower, and the buildings used by the Corporation for a variety of purposes. As well as the stables there was a mortuary and a refuse destructor. The refuse destructor consumed 42-45 tons of refuse daily and generated enough power to operate a pump for street watering, a supply of energy to a stone-breaking plant, and water for the hydraulic power to run the East Hill lift.

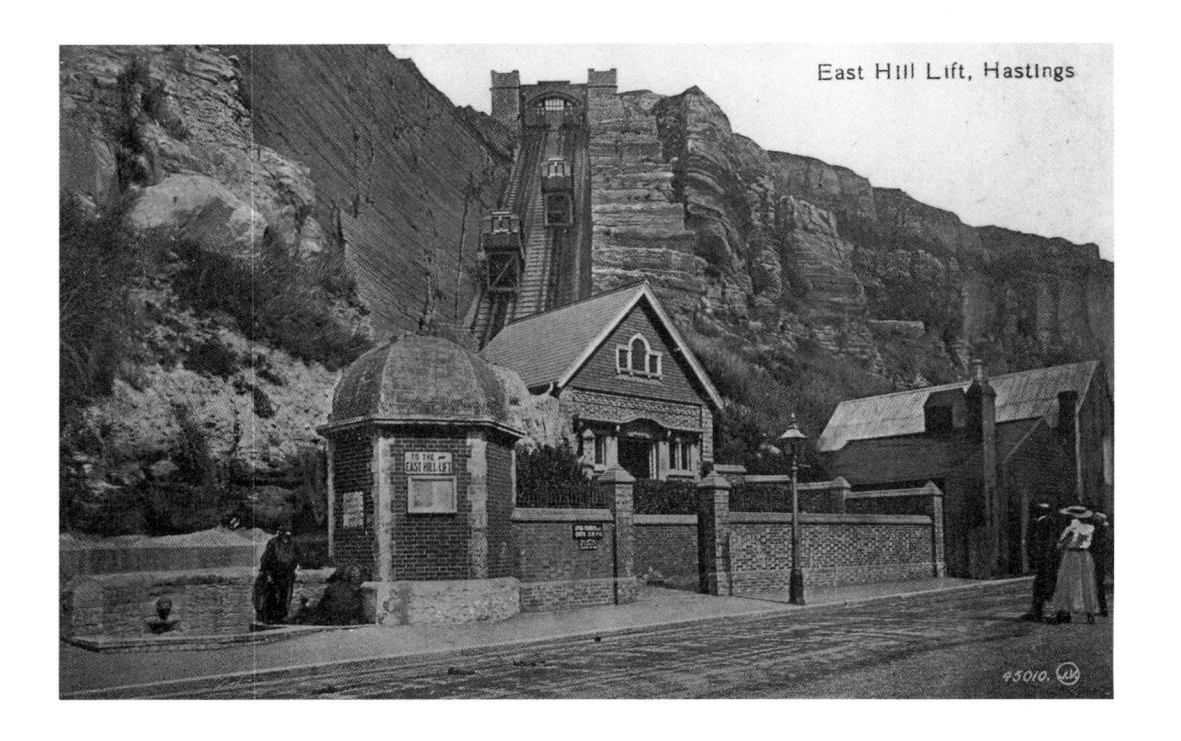

18. c1919. The East Hill lift was opened in 1902 and is still a popular ride with visitors. The brick-domed tank of the East Well was built in 1846 with extra money raised by public subscription for the victims of a fire, which destroyed twenty net shops. It was one of the few sources of fresh water in the Old Town. The building next to the lift is a tanhouse where nets, sails and clothes were tanned.

19. Children collecting water from the East Well in the early 1890s. The cart is delivering nets to the tanhouse.

The Fish Market, Hastings.

20. The retail fishmarket stood at the bottom of High Street until it was demolished in 1928. It was built in 1870, on the traditional site of the fishermen's annual fair. It had twelve stalls when opened, although only four were still in use when it closed in 1924. The space was used as a turning circle for trolley buses from 1928.

21. The wholesale fish market c1904, almost opposite the building in the previous photo. From here barrows would be loaded to sell fish around the town. The buildings in the background are Mercers Bank which stood at the bottom of All Saints Street. By 1895 this area formed the western limit of the fishing industry.

No. 72   THE FISHING QUARTER. HASTINGS

22. Adams and Diton were fish salesmen. The Jolly Fisherman pub has closed, but the London Trader is still there. This picture c1912 shows clearly what a wealth of unique buildings was lost when Mercers Bank was demolished in the 1920s. This also had the effect of moving the fishing industry firmly south of the sea front. The attractive street lamp appears in many of these pictures. In 1910 Hastings had 1595 gas and 615 electric street lamps.

OLD TOWN AND EAST HILL LIFT, HASTINGS.

23. Rock-a-Nore Road about 1930 after Mercers Bank had gone. The Prince Albert pub, next to the imposing shop front of Gallops, Ships Chandlers, below East Cliff House, saw the foundation of the Winkle Club in 1899. 'Breeds Beers', advertised on the side of the building, were brewed in the Old Town for over 100 years.

24. Taken about 1910 this shows the fishmarket and the Lifeboat House which was built in 1882. It was nearly washed away during a storm the following year. In 1959 it was demolished to allow the road to be widened. With the construction of the harbour arm in 1896 the shingle began to build up at this point. The concert party was a popular entertainment for visitors to the seaside until 1940.

25. This picture is dated 5th November 1906 and shows the Hastings lifeboat, Charles Arkcoll II, putting into Rye Harbour after its first rescue mission, to save the crew of a sailing vessel the 'Fruit Girl'.

26. c1928. A web of trolley wires straddles the road, and the lamp standards have changed to accommodate them. Some of these poles with their finials on top can still be seen in the town. The lifeboat can be seen through the open door of the Lifeboat House on the right. The Lifeboat House lost its turret in 1927 to facilitate road widening.

No. 19   THE HARBOUR, HASTINGS.

27. The first recorded attempts at building a harbour were during the reign of Elizabeth I on the rocks shown in this picture taken between 1900-1910. Despite many schemes during the 19th century it was not until 1896 that work began on what is now known as the harbour arm. Work stopped on the project in 1897, when an ancient mud-filled riverbed was found running across the seaward end. The construction caused much conflict with the fishermen. Their net shops and capstans were displaced, and to add insult to injury shingle from their beach was taken for the concrete. Shingle has accumulated against the harbour in recent decades and much of the construction is now buried in the beach.

OLD HASTINGS FROM EAST HILL

28. This view from the East Hill shows the harbour with its railway, soon after work had stopped on its construction, and before all the materials brought in for it had disappeared. Washing can be seen drying on the beach. The wash-house in the Bourne enabled women in the Old Town to make a living by taking in laundry. It was common practice to dry the washing on the beach as few houses had back gardens of any size.

THE HARBOUR, HASTINGS
From the West Hill

29. A final view of the Old Town before we move westwards, c1901. The East Hill lift is under construction and there are piles of building material on the beach for work on the groyne at Rock-a-Nore and the harbour. The tall chimney belongs to the refuse destruction plant. The maze of buildings to the left of the round fishmarket, which formed John Street, Winding Street and East Beach Street were all cleared in the 1930s.

30. Moving along the seafront to the end of George Street c1910. The seafront was then considerably narrower than it is today. The brick building on the left is the Hastings Coastguard Station.

31. Sturdee Place, built in 1902 as the Hastings Coastguard Station and named after a well-known admiral. Coastguards can be seen outside with their families in about 1905. The block is still there, but modern shops disguise the ground floor and the front has been rendered.

32. St. Mary-in-the-Castle is an architectural gem at the heart of Pelham Crescent. Last used as a place of worship in 1978, then left to decay. Restoration work began in 1989. Fund-raising continues to complete the work and equip the building as a performance and visitor centre. A natural spring, an immersion font and catacombs are among the church's unusual features.

33. Caroline Place c1908. The sea came close up here, as shown by the traces of storm damage on the edge of the promenade and the boats drawn well up on the seafront. Only the buildings on the extreme right of the picture in Castle Street still survive.

Hastings Beach

34. The fashions and pleasures of the seaside c1905. From the left we have Denmark Place, Caroline Place, Breeds Place and Pelham Crescent. St. Mary-in-the-Castle is on the right of the picture with Pelham Crescent, these are the only surviving buildings on this stretch of the seafront.

35. The West Hill, a traditional place for cricket practice c1913. The flag marks the top of the lift which rises in a 500ft tunnel from George Street. This lift was opened in 1891.

36. July 5th 1911, the Coronation day of George V and Queen Mary. The West Hill has always been a popular site for celebrations. A huge bonfire has been erected where the children's playground is today. The Naval Volunteer Reserve is firing a salvo.

37. St. Clements Caves, popular with visitors since they were opened to the public in the 1820s. Many local people remember sheltering in them during the Second World War, when they were also used as the Council's record repository. Today much of the natural charm of the caves is hidden by the 'smugglers adventure' now occupying them. The West Hill is said to be riddled with underground passageways.

38. The interior of Hastings Castle has undergone various landscaping schemes since it became a tourist attraction in the 1820s. At the beginning of this century it was laid out as a garden and ivy was allowed to ramble over the masonry. The upkeep of the stonework in this exposed position has been a recurrent problem since Norman times.

39. Wellington Square c1905. The houses here were built from 1815 to accommodate visitors. Assembly Rooms were at the Castle Hotel, on the left of the picture. This was built in 1817, and its demolition in 1966 was another example of the architectural vandalism that has robbed Hastings of many of its best buildings and street scenes. The central garden has lost many of its trees and a new road now cuts across the bottom of the square. From 1920 until the 1950s the square was used as a bus station.

40. Holidaymakers flocking to take to the water c1912. The pleasure yachts were beached by Harold Place and gave a livelihood to many people.

41. The yachts called the 'Albertine' and 'New Albertine' were the most famous of the Hastings pleasure yachts, each one bigger than the last. The first was built in 1865. The second 'Albertine', probably the one shown here was built in 1885 and measured 55ft overall. The 'New Albertine' was built in 1891 and worked as a pleasure yacht until 1924, finishing life as a boulder boat at Newhaven, carrying flints for the china industry. She was one of the biggest boats ever to launch from a beach.

42. The crew of the 'Albertine' opposite the Queens Hotel in 1905. the 'New Albertine' carried 130 passengers, it had a crew of three on board and ten helpers ashore.

HASTINGS. PARADE FROM YACHT POINT.

50393

43. Yacht Point at Harold Place c1920. The capstan is to haul up the pleasure yachts. This was a popular spot for beach photographers and hawkers, catching visitors waiting for a sea trip. The new parade joining White Rock and Denmark Place was built in the 1930s. When rough weather was expected the boats would be hauled well up into Harold Place.

44. c1919. The wreckage of the U-boat mentioned in the message on no. 8. This aerial shot shows the town centre with the Albert Memorial and the Cricket Ground beyond. The railway came to St. Leonards in 1846 but not to Hastings until 1851. The station can be seen top left. The 'New Albertine' pleasure yacht is drawn up on the beach in the centre of the picture.

45. This picture has the caption 'Prehistorics at Hastings Park'. Historical pageants were very popular and often staged as part of local celebrations prior to 1940.

46. c1920. A more peaceful scene in the park, with one of the elegant swan boats emerging from behind the tree. Alexandra Park was opened in 1882 by the Prince and Princess of Wales after whom it was named.

47. A parade in Queens Road c1899, probably Lord John Sanger's Circus. This part of Queens Road was originally known as Bedford Place. St. Andrews Road led up to the church whose striped tower can just be seen on the right of the picture. It was demolished in 1970. The lower part of Queens Road was originally called Meadow Street. In 1876 the street was renamed Queens Road in honour of Queen Victoria. The fine building facing down Queens Road was bombed during the Second World War.

48. Sergeant Buddle with Winifred Pomphrey fitting out the Goldup family with shoes at the Station Road Police Station c1930. Hastings Police ran a benevolent fund to help clothe needy families.

49. The Priory Meadow c1920, before the erection of Marks and Spencer and Queens Parade. The recreation ground was home to Hastings and St. Leonards United Football Club, Hastings Bowls Club and Hastings and St. Leonards Post Office Sports Club in 1910. It was the scene of hustings for elections, military parades and a variety of bizarre happenings, such as the exhibition of a whale's skeleton in 1866 and a tightrope fatality in 1905.

50. The East Sussex Hospital was opened in 1923 and became 'Royal' in the following year. Before the site was infilled with additional hospital buildings, it provided gardens and recreation facilities for staff. The open land in the top left corner is now occupied by the Sports Centre. Below that the building with a cannon in front is John's Place, home of Hastings Museum and Art Gallery since 1928. The Royal East Sussex Hospital was replaced by the Conquest Hospital on the Ridge in 1992.

51. The Albert Memorial clock tower was built in 1863 in memory of Queen Victoria's Consort, Prince Albert. It was 65ft high and soon became the hub of Hastings. Demolished in 1973 after a fire, gone but not forgotten, its name lives on. There is a great variety of public transport in this picture c1905. The trams had a yellow and brown livery. The horse-bus is for a journey along the sea front. Permission for the tram lines to be extended along the sea front was not granted until 1906.

52. This café was a popular venue for morning coffee and afternoon tea with its splendid Art Nouveau shop front in Robertson Street.

53. Robertson Terrace, before its symmetry was spoilt by unsympathetic reconstruction after bomb damage in 1943. In the 1930s the entrance to Europe's first underground car park was excavated in front of the lion. This lion with its matching unicorn at the other end of the green, were reputedly designed by Landseer for Buckingham Palace. These two were surplus to requirements and the Crown Commissioners, who own this land, erected them here. The peaceful parade, ideal for parking a bathchair, became part of the main road.

54. The Palace Hotel, now Palace Chambers, was built in two stages in the 1880/90's. This picture was taken during the First World War when cadets from the Royal Flying Corps were staying there. They can be seen on the balconies and on guard under the imposing portico.

55. White Rock Baths, c1907. Constructed in 1874 with the promenade extending over, it claimed to have the largest swimming bath in the world, the Gentlemen's (tepid) Swim Bath, holding 250,000 gallons of water. There was also a Ladies' Swim Bath and Private 1st and 2nd class Baths. The latter could be hot or cold, fresh or sea water. There were also Turkish baths and a Russian bath. There was one family day and two ladies' days at the baths. Hot, cold or tepid sea water could be delivered to any part of town. A swimming master and a swimming mistress were always in attendance.

56. This bandstand on White Rock Parade was erected in 1895. This picture c1903 shows the promenade packed with deckchairs. The sails of a pleasure yacht can be seen in the background beached at Harold Place.

57. By 1920 the bandstand had been moved to Hastings Pier and been replaced by these kiosks. The names of the shops painted high on the eaves are characteristic of the time, c1927. 'Brown and Woodley' whose name can be seen on the kiosk to the right, and over one of the shops, published a series of postcards from the pictures of W.H. Borrow, a Victorian artist, who lived locally for much of his life.

58. c1905. Hastings Pier opened in 1872, is 910ft long and cost £23,000. The pavilion seated 2,000. It acquired a variety of buildings over the years, and underwent major changes after a serious fire in 1917 when the pavilion at the end was destroyed. It provided a landing stage for pleasure steamers, and had a repertory theatre until the 1960s.

59. A crowded beach scene c1921. The boats belong to Hastings Rowing Club whose headquarters can just be seen under the promenade. It was founded in 1868 and held summer races and an autumn regatta. Rea's Ice Creams, made by an Old Town family, are being sold from a tent near to the Punch and Judy Show. On the pier the pavilion under construction after the 1917 fire can be seen.

60. A view from the pier about 1912 shows the beautiful ironwork and a range of slot machines from scales to 'What the Butler Saw'. Bathing machines can be seen in the distance, the design apparently unchanged since the 1840s. By 1920 they were replaced by bathing cabins.

61. Hastings Pier showing the additions of the 1920s. The decorative ironwork has gone. The bandstand with sheltering wings takes up much of the deck at the inshore end. These side arcades were converted from shelters to small shops in the 1960s. The central bandstand was replaced by the Triodome in 1966 for celebrations of the 1066 anniversary. This has now gone.

62. Naval torpedo boats giving a searchlight display off Hastings Pier during a visit in 1908.

THE PARADE, HASTINGS. (Photographed from an Aëroplane.)

63. An aerial view of the White Rock area pre-1914. The old hospital building (built in 1887) is still opposite the pier and White Rock Road goes straight along the cliff top. The prevailing drift of the shingle from west to east along the beach can be appreciated from this picture.

64. St. Leonards and Hastings were separate towns until they merged during the second half of the 19th century. The Eversfield family acquired the Manor of Gensing, which covered much of St. Leonards, in 1612. The family began to develop their land from the 1850s, joining Burton's St. Leonards to Hastings. This picture, c1907, shows St. Leonards Parade with Eversfield Mansions, a boarding establishment. A branch of the London and South Western Bank is on the western end of this parade of shops.

65. Warrior Square c1907. Like Robertson Terrace the architectural design has suffered in reconstruction after bomb damage. In 1901 the statue of Queen Victoria was erected looking out to sea. No doubt she is unamused at the public toilets erected opposite in the 1990s. A number of street characters are posing for the photographer, including a young boy pushing a milk cart.

66. More milk churns, this time in Warrior Gardens, behind Warrior Square. In 1910 this road boasted two certificated masseuses, a medical electrician and a medical gymnast.

67. The St. Leonards, later the American Palace, Pier, c1905. This was built as a rival to Hastings Pier in 1891 at a cost of £30,000. Situated just west of the Royal Victoria Hotel, its main advantage was that carriages could drive up to the door of the pavilion and patrons were therefore kept dry. The pavilion was smaller than the one on Hastings Pier, seating only 800. In 1940 the pier was breached as a defence measure. It then suffered a fire and was finally demolished in 1951. The paddle steamer has almost certainly been superimposed on this picture for additional interest.

68. St. Leonards Marina c1930 showing the 'Conquerors Stone' in the foreground. First mentioned in 1786, this alleged dining table of William the Conqueror has been moved to and fro along Hastings' sea front over the years. It is currently back in more or less this position.

69. c1905. The Royal Victoria Hotel seen from St. Leonards Pier. James Burton's attractive terraces to the right were replaced by Marine Court in the late 1930s. The buildings on the seaside were known as Royal Victoria Buildings; under the shops were medicinal sea-water baths. They were demolished in the 1940s.

70. c1905. This flower-seller is standing outside Lloyds Bank at 44 Marina, St. Leonards. The canvas on her barrow reads 'Ian Newton, Salesman'.

71. Summerfields built by the Brisco family in the 1830s, a school from before the First World War until 1960, then demolished to make way for civic offices. Some of its garden features can still be seen in the woods behind the Magistrates Court.

GENERAL VIEW, ECCLESBOURNE, HASTINGS.

72. c1910. Ecclesbourne Glen with a coastguard and the coastguard cottages in the centre of the picture. The rifle butts can be seen on the far hillside, constructed for the local rifle volunteer corps which was incorporated into the 5th (Cinque Ports) Battalion of the Royal Sussex Regiment in 1908. Cultivated plots are visible up the left side of the glen. These were known as the 'Strawberry Fields'. The coastguard cottages were demolished in 1961 when the cliff edge had almost reached them. The coastal erosion this century has been dramatic as this picture well illustrates.

GENERAL VIEW OF CLIVE VALE

73. Posted 1907 showing Harold Road, Godwin Road and Clive Vale Schools. The track leading from Harold Road up the side of the hill, where Gurth Road is today, was a private road to the golf club. The glass houses on the westside of Harold Road belong to Gilbert's Nursery. Clive Vale was developed in the 1870-80s.

74. Laying the tramlines at the junction of Old London, Saxon and Offa Roads, opposite Christ Church Ore in 1905. The corrugated iron meeting room can be seen to the right of the church. The bus is a demonstration model Thornycroft which was operating with the Hastings and St. Leonards Omnibus Company for a few months.

75. Bliss's Nursery in Fairlight Road, Ore, just above the junction with Middle Road c1908. The width of the road remains unchanged but now it has street lamps.

Ore Place (Hastings).

76. Ore Place built in 1863 by Thomas Spalding. On the right can just be seen part of the enlargements made by a Jesuit Order after they took the building over in 1905. The buildings were used as an Army Record Office from 1940. They were demolished in 1987.